<u>GIRL BOSS:</u>

An Inspirational Guide to Building Your Brand and Manifesting Your Dreams

Yasmin Watts

Publisher's Note: This is a work of fiction, names, characters, places and incidents are either the product of
the author's imagination, or are used fictitiously, and any resemblance to actual persons, living or dead,
business establishment, events, or locales is entirely coincidental.

eBook Edition: Abstract Village, 2019

Print Edition: Abstract Village, 2019

ISBN: 9781710092516

GIRL BOSS / YASMIN WATTS – 1st ed.

Cover Art and Design: Gabe Rios

Photos: Drea Nicole

[?]

My Inspiration:

m completely inspired by Oprah and Iyanla Vanzant. I love who they are and what they resent... powerful and impactful women of color. They remind me that there is a story behind ery individual who has ever succeeded and gotten to where they are today. At some point in eir lives someone told them no, someone rejected them, and support was lacking. It all stoked eir fire to keep pushing.

e also found inspiration in Necole Kane's story of hitting "rock bottom." I think people forget at we are all human and no one person is perfect. It's okay to fail, it's okay to be imperfect d it's really ok to "hit rock bottom" as long as you fight to stand again. ▢

Foreword to the Author (Edwina Price)

She is a QUEEN, in competition with no one other than herself. She pushes herself to be a better version daily, so much so, that she once lost herself in the process. That was her only weakness. She quickly recognized her need for balance, and now strides in perfect harmony with the universe. She carries herself with dignity and an insurmountable amount of class. She balances being a single mother, dedicated family member, companion and friend – all while working full-time and managing successful businesses. If you are unclear as to what a Girl Boss might look like, Yasmin L. Watts exudes every characteristic of a GIRL BOSS!

To know Yasmin today, you would never believe the story of how we became friends. A neighborhood dispute-that no one to this day can recall in its origin-was the beginning of a beautiful friendship. I guess the best description of our relationship is: we are enemies turned close life-long friends. I affectionately called her Lil Southside or Baby Watts.

We come from humble beginnings. Although we attended different middle schools, we spent much time together in the "trailer park" where we grew up. My parents trusted her parents enough to let my brother and I spend the night often (hunny, they trusted no one outside of family). Her family became mine, and vice versa. We made a great deal of childhood memories in that park. Those thick glasses of hers killed the game!

High school brought us even closer. We hooped together, went to church together, and ran the streets together. Yasmin was always strong in her faith, and always had an encouraging word. Fun fact about Yasmin: in her youth, she wrote two gospel songs that were actually pretty good! So, it did not surprise me when I learned the tone of this book.

Yasmin began college a year before I enrolled and when I stepped foot on campus, we took the intramural basketball court and party scene by storm. We continued to make great memories until I encountered a major life lesson, and out of shame distanced myself from Yasmin. Years passed, but Yasmin NEVER changed. She remained loyal to our friendship through the test of uncertainty, distance and time. When Yasmin moved to Atlanta, our communication increased. I never felt indifferent about our friendship and there was always so much love when we saw each other. Years passed and life happened. Yasmin became pregnant; Camden literally had an army of aunts and uncles. I admired Yasmin's strength as a mother. She continued working and taking college courses while dealing with the stress of life. When I became a mother two years later, I grew a new-found respect for Yasmin as a mother and young woman.

emember being in an unhealthy relationship while becoming a new mother to an infant. I was
a new city, miles away from family without any support. I reached out to Yasmin. Without
sitation she provided a level of warmth that literally saved my life. Since that time, our
ationship has grown immensely, and we are on this life journey together! It has been a
vilege to share life with such a beautiful soul.

smin moves different. She possesses so much dope-ness, is spiritually grounded, and is
deniably the most selfless person I know. She has so much discipline that procrastination has
room in her life. Yasmin dominates anything she does. She is a self-motivated, empowered,
dacious GIRL BOSS...unapologetically.

ope that you are blessed by her book, it's jammed packed with inspiration and interactive
ols that will aid you, on your path to becoming a GIRL BOSS!

Acknowledgements:

Camden

To my son Camden "Cam": kid you just don't know how much of a light you are in this world. You are truly my pride and joy. Thank you for believing in mommy and understanding the hustle and the grind. Everything I do is for you and best believe we are going to WIN baby!

Kinia and Theo

The power couple of all power couples. There are not enough pages in a book, minutes in a movie or time in a day to tell you both how much I love and appreciate you...past the moon and back again. There are so many lives that the both of you have impacted and literally saved. You are providers, even when what you have is your last to give. I tell you often that I don't know how I could ever repay you, but I pray that God places me in a position to give you back double.

Kinia, thank you for this vision, for lighting the fire for this book and for believing in your baby girl.

Mama

Doshia Mae! Hunnie when they say "I don't know where I would be without my praying Mama" I feel that all in my spirit!!! Mama you taught me how to survive through the struggle and that real talk. You taught me how to develop my own relationship with God and you've prayed for me even in times when I couldn't pray for myself. I admire your strength, your courage, and your faith so much. Lord knows our family has been through the trenches and we've certainly taken some losses. Yet, we've still managed to make it through. Thank you for giving me the foundation to trust God and have faith...in and through all circumstances. I love you!

Jay

Babe, I don't know where to begin. Thank you for coming into my life and loving me and the kid truly, genuinely, and unconditionally. Through the ups and downs of this crazy life we remain solid. I'm so thankful for the thousands of ways you provide support even in times when "support" simply means showing up. I know that God has amazing things on the horizon for our family and I cannot wait to see what the future holds.

ch and Porscha (Avery's parents)

y brother, my brother. Growing up we used to" fight like cats and dogs", but hey that's
mily! Fast forward...we are all grown up now and boy do we go hard for our village. Thank you
 stepping up and being an amazing uncle and father figure even beyond your ordinary
ligation. You trusted the process of life, and oh what a man you've become.

rscha I'm truly grateful that God granted Zach the opportunity to bring you into our lives. You
ve blessed us with your presence, support, and unwavering love in more ways than one.

ve you both more than words can express.

y DOPE Ass Tribe

an, where would I be without ya'll?! I can't imagine this life without the moments we have
ared, laughed, cried, had kids, the whole nine. You couldn't tell us anything back in those
ys and look at us now. Twenty years and counting... and we are still rocking the same. I can't
l you all enough how much I love you; for being there for me and for always stepping in with
e kid. Real friends are hard to come by. I'm truly blessed that ours has stood the test of time.
ould literally write a separate book on our friendships and bond alone, but y'all already know.
e time for God; for positioning us in the way that HE has, for working in and through us, and
 preparing us for the next level. When ONE WINs, WE ALL WIN!

avia

my "Suh" and my baby before my own baby. I hope in reading this you see just how much
u mean to me baby girl. I don't call you "Suh" in casual fashion. It's my personal term of
dearment for the one who has been my rider since I can remember. No amount of age
ference could prove our love any differently. Listen baby girl, I need you to stay focused and
 for everything God has for you. I love you and I'm rooting extra hard for you!

. Carol

 love you Gigi! God has truly blessed our lives with your presence. One thing for certain and
o things for sure, you have never left our side. Thank you for always being there through the
od, bad and indifferent. You have always showed genuine love and support and no amount
words could ever thank you enough. I am and will always be forever grateful.

ps (James O.)

iting this one hurts. The pain of your loss still has a devastating impact on my life. You were
 from a perfect man, but you were "Daddy". Losing you taught me to never take anything in
 for granted. Life, I've discovered, is way too short. If I didn't understand that before your
ath, I have certainly felt that afterwards.

You fought so hard daddy, even up to your last days, even beyond your soul growing weary. This one is for you; a true soldier and fighter. No matter what life throws at me, I pray I can face it with your level of strength and resilience. Hug Mama (Grandma Francis) for me and tell Granddaddy we miss him and those blow pops. You are and forever will be loved and missed.

Everyone

Man, oh man! I know some of you are going to be mad at me for not saying a word about this process. What I've learned is that success often calls for you to sometimes move in silence.

This was a time when I needed to focus on me, with minimum influence from the outside world.

To be honest I don't think my mom even knew. During so many conversations with family and friends I wanted to "spill the beans"; however, each time I felt God whispering, "not yet". So, I waited…patiently and obediently. Now we are here.

Of course, if you're reading this, then I can officially announce that ya girl is a published author

This was never one of my initial life goals, but God has plans for my life that are so much bigger than my own.

Whatever HE has in store, I'm coming for it ALL.

⁇

Girl Check Yourself Before You Wreck Yourself

nce read a quote that said, "the Universe can only be as good to you as you are to yourself."

hoa...talk about deep. My friends and I talk constantly about living a purposeful life and one

th intention. In October of 2018, about 20 or more so women joined together for a "Bikes

d Brunch" event to celebrate my birthday. The group was intentional in making sure I truly

joyed the occasion and the experience. That meant staying off my phone (which my

yfriend mentions quite often), escaping social media, and for about three uninterrupted

urs, not focusing on anything other than what was happening in the moment...reconnection,

terhood, friendship.

eir good intentions turned out to be a blessing that I didn't even realize I needed. As a mom-

eneur, I am constantly living life on the go. Life as a whole is a constant battle with me trying

balance my 9 to 5 while also managing two businesses, raising a 9-year-old son, and finding

ys to equally distribute attention among my relationships: partner, son, family, and friends.

esh, with all of that I failed to mention time for ME.

December of 2018, I was completely adamant about giving myself a break. I realized that I

s giving so much of myself to others that I truly had nothing left for me. I felt myself on the

ge of a mental breakdown and for the first time ever, I felt depleted of my mental and

ysical capacities. I knew that if I did not give myself time to breathe and recharge, I would

ak at any given moment. Yes, it was that serious.

I did the unthinkable. I gave myself permission to take a break. A real break. I went on

cation, turned down projects (even ones with lucrative potential), and I simply said "no".

ile it was one of the hardest decisions I've ever had to make, taking that much-needed time

s instrumental in saving my sanity. As stressed as I was, it's not an exaggeration to say that

ing that time off literally saved my life.

*****

One of my best friends, Edwina Price, has a personal health and wellness blog entitled <u>"How is The Health Did That Happen?"</u>. The blog focuses on mental health, physical health, and overall wellness. The more I've read her articles and posts, the more I've found myself in tune with what living life intentionally and on purpose means "for me."

I recently sent my friends a message asking them to send me two qualities about myself that inspires them and one additional characteristic or quality that I could improve upon. The responses were far more gracious than I imagined they would be. Reading their responses enabled me to see myself through their eyes. "Genuinely supportive", "selfless", "a pure heart" Wow talk about tear jerkers right.

Doing that assessment helped me to also come to terms with what I already knew internally...that I often sacrifice my happiness for others. As I reflected on those moments where I was the selfless, supportive, "be there in the midnight hour" kind of friend, I also realized that in many of those moments I gave up something to be so... mostly time and energy.

To be considered a "true" friend, I did what we've been taught and molded to do...give, give, and give some more. Even when my own emotions were unbalanced, when my own motivations were low, or my own reserves were running on empty, I gave. Even when my own baggage was crowding my mental space, I shoved it all to the side and gave. I gave...until I literally gave out! My internal resources were depleted and a complete and utter break-down seemed imminent.

Never again.

I'm learning (slowly but surely) how to get back to my true self. I'm big on "manifestation" and started writing down the things in which I wanted to manifest. I stopped expecting things to just happen and I learned to allow God's timing to work on my own behalf. I have engaged in

e daily practice of dedicating time to reading my devotionals, listening to inspirational music,
eaking positive affirmations and protecting my peace. In other words, I'm practicing self-love.
 working on me, giving more of myself to myself so that I can give the best of "me" to
hers. By that same token, I am also working on not stretching myself too thin.

us far, I am happy with the direction in which my life is going. For the first time in a LONG
ne, I believe that everything I am manifesting and everything I am believing to come true,
I. It's been a long and often overwhelming process...one in which I've had to face reality with
ew things. Yet, I finally feel that the universe is aligning, and things are finally falling into
ce.

 a crazy, beautiful journey. The time is NOW for your journey to begin!

xo
smin Watts

The Inspirational Journey

Welcome to this journey of prayer, manifestation and restoration. Throughout this journey, you will learn to speak life and manifest the things in which you are hoping for and praying for. Like anything else, it takes work and commitment. If you are intentional and specific with your prayers, nothing is impossible. The key to receiving, is believing.

What does it mean exactly to manifest? To manifest something is to bring something forth into your physical life experience by using your thoughts, feelings, and beliefs.

This thought process is nothing new, and it's certainly not rocket science. By now you've heard through several sources and people that the power of transformation begins within YOU. TED Talks are presented with that message, transformational speakers are preaching that message, a hundred books have been written expressing that same message.

It all means one thing...training your mind and conscious to focus specifically on those things you want to have or to happen in your real life. For instance, if you have been constantly wanting a new job, new car, or even a new relationship, you would project your thoughts and focus on those specific things utilizing techniques such as meditation and visualization.

In layman's terms, the concept of manifestation involves the idea that the universe, God, and the earth are not only spiritual concepts but active energies and forces at work in our daily lives. If your mind is trained and focused on specific, targeted goals, then in theory, your mental resources are calling upon the energies of those forces and channeling them towards those goals until they actually "manifest" in your reality.

Sounds crazy right? In truth, most of us utilize some form of this every day. Think about the age-old practice of praying. We pray believing that God (or Godly figure) has the power to transform our prayers into very real concepts. The art of manifestation is very similar to this practice.

hat exactly does that mean and how do you even begin? In truth, if it was really all that

nple, we would all be millionaires!

the end of the day, the practice of manifestation alone is not enough to put that new car in

ur garage or lay the foundation on that new house. Manifestation needs ACTION to follow.

u have to put in the work of completing applications, saving for down payments and creating

dgets. Manifestation simply trains your mind to not only focus on setting goals, but the

tions needed to see them come to fruition.

The Art of Manifestation

Personal Task: Before getting started on your inspirational journey, think about all of the things you want to achieve in your life. Taking a few minutes to answer the following questions will serve as your first official steps toward manifesting your dreams to your reality.

STEP 1: What are the specific things I want to manifest in my life?

STEP 2: What specific obstacles can I identify that would keep me from manifesting my dreams

***Do yourself a huge favor Sis and get really REAL on this one. Obstacles can come in many forms including tangible ones such as money but can also be people or circumstances. Don't underestimate the impact negative energy and toxic people can have on whether or not you succeed.

STEP 3: What ACTIONS can I take towards manifesting my dreams?

***Again, be specific. For example: If your work schedule is getting in the way of you accomplishing your personal goals, start thinking about a real plan to gain some of your time back such as transitioning to a part-time position.

Setting Specific Goals

fore beginning your personal journey, I want you to ask yourself a very important question:
at is your endgame? Meaning, where exactly are you trying to go, what exactly are you
ing to achieve, and what specifically are you wanting to accomplish?

is may seem like a menial task, but I assure you that it's a relevant one.

rsonally, I struggled with that one question for years. Here's what I was clear on: I knew I
nted wealth, I knew I wanted to be a successful entrepreneur, and I knew I wanted financial
bility for myself and my son.

at all sounds good; however, when you really dig beneath the surface, it all seems rather
gue. Financial stability is one thing...having enough money for my son to go to college, to
rchase a home, and having the ability to set clear financial yearly goals, is entirely different.
ing a successful entrepreneur sounded like a great goal to put on the list. That is until I
rted thinking about what specific businesses I wanted to dive into. Since I wasn't clear on the
e of business(es) I wanted to venture into, how could I be clear on the amount of funds I
eded for an initial investment or how those businesses would fit into my overall brand.

e lesson I learned was an essential one: if you don't know where you're going or even "why",
 path to getting there will be even less clear.

now that it's time for you to set your personal goals down on record, you may be wondering
w to ensure that your goals are relevant to achieving the outcomes you want.

ant to share a tool or rather a method with you that I have incorporated into my own
sonal practice and is widely used in the areas of project management, employee
formance management and personal development.

Setting S.M.A.R.T Goals:

S(Specific) **M**(Measurable) **A**(Attainable) **R**(Realistic) **T**(Time-bound)

Specific	• Your goal should be clear, detailed and explain exactly what you are going to do and how.
Measurable	• Your goal should be measurable. A tangible measure will help determine how successful you were with your goal.
Achievable	• Your goal must be achievable and help motivate you to suceed. Impossible goals will only demotivate you. _
Relevant	• Your goal must coincide with your overall objective and fit in with the bigger picture.
Timely	• Your goal should have a set timeline with specific start and end dates so your goal is set in stone and set to be delivered.

Following this guideline will help you establish goals that are well-defined, relevant to your purpose, and achievable. It's then a call to action and not just a meaningless, daily chore.

Unleash your inner BOSS!!!

rsonal Task: Set 15 specific goals in all areas of your life. No goal is too big or too small and member to BE SPECIFIC. (i.e. if you want a car.... red car? Mercedes Benz?) —

t 30 mins of quiet time aside to write down your goals and revisit them every day. Say them ud. Remember your dreams and goals can't work unless you do.

Personal Goals:

_____

_____

_____

_____

_____

_____

_____

_____

_____

_____

_____

_____

_____

_____

_____

Restoration

Women, as a whole, typically have this deep desire to nurture and love others. What happens all too often is that we end up losing a piece of ourselves along the way. This was my exact state when I was at the point of giving, giving, and giving.

Be confident in knowing you can restore yourself and live the rest of your life feeling fully empowered in who you are.

The process of restoration involves re-connecting your body, mind, and spirit. The focus is on creating a healthy lifestyle coupled with a stronger knowing of self. When you tend to your inner-most needs, you create the opportunity to reconnect with your most powerful self.

We think we have to do it all, and we often feel shame when our bodies and minds tell us...or yet, show us...that we can't! There's truth in the saying that "you can't pour from an empty cup." You're not doing yourself justice if you don't create time to replenish and restore your soul and spirit. Your mental and physical health demand that you do!

Personal task: Make it a daily habit to focus on RESTORATION. Begin the journey with 5 minutes of silence and meditation, then slowly increase your time and include more personal methods.

What are some of your favorite SELF CARE activities? Make a commitment to engage in at least one per week.

Intentional Prayer

rayer is just being intentional about your conversation with God"-unknown

specific and intentional when you pray. Don't be afraid to ask BIG. Instead of focusing on the
in of current circumstances, stand on the promises that God has for your life. When one
ays with intention, one gets God's attention. When one gets God's attention, one will be clear
out God's instructions.

5 Keys to Praying Intentionally

Take action in prayer with a heart open to God.
Look to benefit others.
Take responsibility.
Focus on a promise.
Respond with joy.

ou could pray for **ONE THING** and know that it would make a significant, lasting, possibly life-
changing difference in your life, what would you pray for?

_____

_____

_____

_____

_____

_____

_____

_____

Affirmations

"It's not what you say out of your mouth that determines your life; it's what you whisper to yourself that has the most power."– Robert Kiyosaki

Using positive affirmations as a form of self-care works! As the burning of sage is utilized to clear out the negative energy of spaces, affirmations, when routinely used, help to clear out the self-sabotaging, negative thoughts that too often plague our psyche and impacts our sense of "self."

From birth the world seeks to define who we are. We are born a specific gender, in a specific socio-economic class, of a specific race in a specific geographical location. From this, we as humans make deductions and judgements about other humans. And we as a people are not always kind. As a woman I've had to deal with the unfair stereotypes the world places on me. I'm defined as inferior and worthless. I'm objectified and abused. And that's simply being born a woman. As a Black woman I'm viewed as even less.

Added to those challenges are the increasing pressures stemming from media and social media platforms that have us defining the quality of our lives based on images depicted on our phones, computer screens, and other devices. Our sense of self-worth now correlates with how well we're "keeping up with the Jones" or at least how good we can pretend we are and how many "likes" and hearts we can accumulate in an hour's time. It's a crazy trap that we continuously fall into.

That's why it's so important for the world not to be the loudest voice speaking to your soul and spirit. Speak over yourself...encourage yourself...motivate yourself. LOVE yourself. Affirmations not only plant the seeds of enrichment, abundance, health, and prosperity, but they also nourish them to their full potential. Speak it...visualize it...and watch it MANIFEST!

Personal Task: What are some of your daily affirmations? Today come up with at least 5.

I AM...

_____

_____

_____

_____

_____

There are times when the Storm will Rage!!!

In the spiritual battles of life, we must remember that when God works hard, the devil works even harder. Over the last four years, I've really grown in my walk with God and I have truly come to understand what it means to go into the "War Room."

To share a personal experience, a few years ago I was going through a very intense and frustrating time at work. My teammates and I were struggling with being "perfect" and simply being "good enough" for my then manager. Our entire team constantly felt demeaned, always felt as though our jobs were at stake, and continually felt wholly incompetent. I found myself a situation where I truly hated my job and I literally felt like my work life was hell.

For much too long I allowed my peace to go disturbed. I was spiritually shook!

During that time, I made one of the biggest decisions ever in my life. With only my resignation letter and my faith in God, I took a leap of faith and resigned from my position. I was a single mom with no back up plan; however, I instantly felt so much weight lifted off my shoulders. At that moment at least one battle was no longer mine to fight.

It was during that personal trial when I retreated to my War Room the most: to pray for myself, my coworkers and what was even a surprise to me, my manager. At the time, my mom provided me with several bible verses that I would stick in my bible with my managers' name inscribed on them. Every night I was in my War Room reading my scriptures and just praying. Having my own pep talks, I would always tell myself "God sits high and looks low. He knows everything I'm going through and he's working behind the scenes for my good."

And He was.

My work situation changed. When I started down that path my whole intent was to resign. However, I rescinded my letter after promises from upper management that changes were in e works. Initially I had my doubts but once again I went into warfare, prayed, and that inner ice calmed my spirit and said, "be still". It took less than 30 days for a transformation to cur. The weapon that had been formed against me did not prosper; eventually it was moved altogether! Not only had God worked out that situation, but internally I felt the print of his work in me as I noticed a shift in my mood and spirit. For months I had been in ch a negative head space. My spirit was defeated, and my mind had been in a constant state turmoil. After prayer, meditation, and transformation, peace had once again become my mpanion.

metimes I wonder what would've happened if I'd never moved my feet, if I would've never pped out on faith with my bold resignation attempt.

nat life has taught me is that God sometimes places us in situations to strengthen us and to th test and build our character. God has brought me through before, and I must continue to ist and have faith that He will undoubtedly bring me through again and again.

arned some valuable life lessons during that time:

- Storms are growing pains. Long before we enter a storm, God already knows how he is going to bring us out.
- God's purpose for us is greater than our problems and our pain.
- God uses storms as reminders to show us just how powerful He is.
- Don't panic when God is quiet. As the saying goes "the teacher is always quiet during a test".

Celebrate Your Small Victories

Raise your hand if you've ever felt like a complete failure. You can't see it, but mine are once again raised high to the sky. Even with being a successful entrepreneur and making profession strides on my full-time job, I still have feelings of doubt, insecurity, and incompetence. No matter what I do right, that subconscious voice somehow finds its way in…nagging and whispering about all the things I've done wrong (my perception at least) or haven't managed t accomplish.

There was a time in my life when that voice was extra loud. So loud that positive affirmations had no room to settle in and grow. I was running around like a "jack of all trades", desperately trying to find balance among the many roles and hats I was wearing. That juggling act was not proving to be successful. I still felt as though I was coming up short and that my son, my job n partner and my family were continually being short-changed. I needed 36 hours in a day inste of 24! There was never enough time and each new day bore new personal and professional tasks to add to the ever-growing to-do list. I was so caught up in my own negativity that I faile to acknowledge my own self-worth. It was a dangerous mind-set. Depression and anxiety became all too real aspects of my daily life.

Here's what I learned: if we aren't mindful, we can succumb to that voice and never fulfill our promised purpose nor full potential. I knew I had to change my entire mental state, and only then could I even begin to change my reality. I began reading self-help and inspirational books became inspired and motivated by stories of other people, especially women, who were struggling at this life thing just as I was. I learned to affirm myself and started doing daily devotionals to nourish my mind, body and spirit. I began to become more mindful of my daily speak and actions. As I did so, I became more aware of just how much negativity I was allowir to take up space in my world. No more!

A change had come, and transformation was on its way! I learned to celebrate myself and in doing so, became more open and mindful of celebrating my small victories as well as my bigg es. I celebrated the five tasks I somehow managed to scratch off my to-do list instead of cusing on the thirty more waiting for my attention. I started celebrating getting my son to hool on time (oh the struggle is real) instead of being angry about the effort it took to do so. an entrepreneur, celebrating small victories are important as well. My sister is a writer and an does she celebrate if she manages to get even one page written in a day's time.

ost people are uncomfortable with celebrating their small victories. It may seem trivial to lebrate something as seemingly unimportant as packing a healthy lunch or even ironing hool clothes for the next day for instance.

wever, you're not necessarily celebrating the achievement itself; you're celebrating your bits. You're celebrating the good behavior and the person you're becoming. If you don't use to appreciate your little victories – if you're simply rushing from one task to another – en it's easier to become exhausted and demotivated. That's not a good state to be in.

go ahead Sis...celebrate you! You are worthy! You're perfectly imperfect!

tend yourself a little bit of grace. Give yourself a pat on the back because whether you knowledge it or not, you accomplished SOMETHING today. And that is always worth a ebration.

re are some ways you can become more conscious in celebrating the small victories:

Feel the Excitement

th each little win, you're getting closer to your goal. Let that thought excite you! Don't save ur excitement for the "big" things; celebrate each step that you take.

2.   Treat Yourself

Every achievement, regardless of its size, deserves a reward. Whether it's cooking your favorite meal, watching a fun movie, or purchasing some new clothes, you should always take the time to reward yourself. (I must say I've struggled with this one!)

3.   Share Your Wins

Be proud of your achievements and speak about them with fulfillment and enthusiasm. When you verbalize your wins, you're reinforcing them, and this should motivate you to continue. Sharing your wins may also inspire others to reach for their goals as well – so everybody wins

Personal Task: Take a moment to reflect on the past week! What are some of your small victories?

⬚

Reflection

too often we get caught up in the troubles or busy-ness of our daily lives. Making mistakes, ssing a deadline for a high-pressured project, or not getting something accomplished from e never-ending to-do list can seem like the end of the entire world. It can be overwhelming d manifest itself in ways that are detrimental to our overall health: panic attacks, depression, art palpitations, or in my own case, debilitating migraines and high levels of anxiety.

we take a minute to step back, reflect on those issues, and breathe, we'll realize that in the and scheme of things those seemingly big things aren't that grand after all. I'm sure you've ard the saying "don't sweat the small stuff". Yes, it's a cliché; however, it's a small rule that uld have a huge impact on the overall quality of your life. It can calm us down and lower our ess levels. We gain perspective, and that's a good thing.

rsonal Task: Take a few moments today to reflect on some important life questions. Give urself at least 90 seconds for each question.

How do I want to grow?

_____

_____

_____

_____

_____

2.   What would I want to experience in life if time and money were not an issue?

_____

_____

_____

_____

_____

3. Where am I going? How do I want to be remembered when I am gone?

_____

_____

_____

_____

_____

What do I want to contribute to this world?

_____

_____

_____

_____

_____

If I achieved all of my life's goals, how would I feel?

_____

_____

_____

_____

Preparation

There's a widely used quote from NFL coach Jimmy Johnson which states "success is what happens when opportunity meets preparation". In life, and particularly in the world of entrepreneurship, no truer words were ever spoken.

Everything we've talked about so far has been some form of preparation. Manifestation, affirmation, reflection, meditation and prayer are all tools to prepare and align your mind, body and spirit. These daily practices and habits are there to fall back on during those moments when the storm is raging full force and you can't seem to get your bearing in life.

Just as winter prepares plants and trees for warmer weather, a spiritually dormant season is a time of preparation—when our inner character is developed and strengthened. Strong character is essential for withstanding storms that come during seasons of growth and harvest.

In case you missed it, let me sneak it in one more time: seasons of growth AND harvest. That entire concept is essential to grasp. God has a way of preparing us for growth and harvest. To have seasons of growth, you must first plant seeds. Likewise, seasons of harvest cannot be accomplished without ACTION!

All too often we get stuck in preparation mode. We fear being great, we fear the unknowns and the what ifs. We fear failure, ridicule, and not living up to the expectations of others. This causes us to remain dormant far longer than we should. God nudges us outside of our comfort zones toward unfamiliar experiences to encourage us to rely on Him. And all too often, we try to hang on to what is familiar before we have confidence that the new thing is right for us. Don't get me wrong, it's important to research and plan, but at some point, you have to take that knowledge and actually put it to use. A vision board is just a decorated piece of cardboard unless you take the necessary action steps to achieve those goals. You can write a thousand words on paper, but if you never take the steps to be published, then all you have is a journal of dreams. Unpicked fruit spoils on the vine much as unyielded crops wither and die. A dream deferred will eventually die.

od has amazing plans for our lives, and He wants us to fulfill our dreams and live lives filled th blessings, hopes and promises. You will get there—if you are willing to do your part and ust God to do His.

e more you lean on and trust in Him through that process, the sooner you'll be ready for natever He has prepared for you.

s HARVEST time Sis!

t's get everything He promised us!

Personal Task: Today, take 5 minutes to reflect on your specific goals and write a letter to yourself about how God is preparing you to reach those goals!

Dear _____,

_____

_____

_____

_____

_____

_____

_____

_____

_____

_____

_____

_____

You got this girl!

_____

Signature

Bet on...Yourself!

all realness…. Making the decision to become an Entrepreneur is a whole different level of stepping out on faith. You have to be willing to commit, invest and take a loss even if no one else does… you gotta be willing to bet on yourself!" - Yasmin Watts

told you I haven't taken a few losses I would be straight up lying. I knew that making the cision to become an entrepreneur would in no way be easy. In fact, I knew that the process uld involve a lot of sacrifice. Of course, I didn't exactly know what that sacrifice would entail til I took a leap of faith.

arted my photography business, Yasmin Watts Photography, just few short years ago. I gan by taking personal pictures for family and friends or on occasions at random events. at in turn led to my partner and I having a conversation as to whether I would ever seriously nsider evolving my hobby into an actual business or just have it remain as an active side stle. Christmas of that year, he invested in me by gifting me my very own professional mera. Thus began the very real process of taking my talents to the next level.

t, even as people began to book me, I still suffered from insecurity, believing that I was where near the level of other photographers in the Atlanta area. Initially I shied away from ing major events or booking upscale clients. Fear of failure kept me grounded and stuck.

I ventured more into the industry, however, I began to develop my own lane and my brand veloped. My work was becoming more identifiable and creative. More and more people gin to take a chance on me and almost every client returned to either book me for additional ents or refer me to others. From then on, I knew that if people were willing to take a chance me then I was willing to "bet on myself!"

*****

Fast forward to the spring of 2018. I started thinking of ways to develop multiple streams of income. It was important to me that whatever I ventured into be more than just another business. I wanted something meaningful, something people could relate to and something that I was passionate about. It was at that time that the idea was born to infiltrate the world of ethnic head wraps.

As a creative and photographer, I had fallen in love with beautiful women adorning head wraps in gorgeous, diverse prints. The images I witnessed were regal and stunning. So, I decided to create my own brand of head wraps, Issa Wrap Inspired Collection. Issa Wrap Inspired Collection is more than just a brand. My overall goal is for it to serve as an empowering platform for women. Each wrap tells a signature story and is inspired by powerful, influential women from my personal life, media, politics and other areas. There's one named after my grandmother and even one inspired by First Lady (she always will be) Michelle Obama. It's an incredible feeling when people write or speak to me about their personal connection to a wrap or how they love the inspiration behind a particular product. That brand has now expanded to include jewelry and wraps for toddlers and kids. With that being said, I can officially declare it certified SUCCESS.

I survived all of those moments of doubts, insecurities and second-guessing myself. I had bet on myself...and won!

It's been a blessing and a pain to grow and develop as a profitable business owner, but I wouldn't change it for nothing. I'm building my brand, but more importantly, I'm creating a legacy and a blueprint for my son. He's by my side as I work countless hours beyond my full-time job. He's right there with me helping to pack, tag and fulfill orders. He's been with me on shoots and even has his own aspirations to model, act, and write his own book!

cause I dared to believe...he dares to DREAM! So, it appears I'm doing something right after

Protecting Your Peace... At All Costs

"Peace. It does not mean to be in a place where there is no noise, trouble, or hard work. It means to be in the midst of those things and still be calm in your heart." -Unknown

We as human beings, underestimate how much we allow the happenings of the outside world to affect us inside. The iconic poet Maya Angelou is quoted with the saying "Don't bring negative to my door." She strongly believed in protecting your space as negative energy will somehow find ways to invade your physical surroundings, but seep into the very core of your inner being.

Diligently seek inner peace and protect it from all that may mean you no good. Being negative or finding something to be negative about is easy but the true test of character and growth is when you can remain a source of positivity even in the chaos and beauty of the struggle.

Today, no matter what may be going on around you or what you may be faced with, trust and understand that your "peace" is more important; whatever "peace" means to you. Love yourself enough to put your peace first. Love yourself enough to treat yourself. You don't deserve to feel less than. You don't have to measure up to the expectations others place on you. Love yourself enough to have standards. Give yourself permission to walk away from any person or situation that does not uphold those standards...even if that means releasing the bonds of family and/or friendships.

Growth and success can sometimes be a painful and lonely process. Especially when you begin to realize that not everyone is meant to take that journey with you. If you know anything about plants, then you know that in order for new stems to sprout, you must first rid the plant of its dead leaves. This allows for space and resources to support the new growth. Such is the case real life. We can't access the path to success because negativity, chaos and dysfunction are blocking the way. Our energy and focus are being diverted from their true purpose. It's the ultimate illusion and smokescreen.

and your ground! Shake loose negativity, beat back abuse, stomp down insecurity. You are valuable and worthy of protection.

When God Makes You Uncomfortable

"For I know the thoughts that I think toward you, says the Lord, thoughts of peace and not of evil, to give you a future and a hope. Then you will call upon me and go and pray to me, and I will listen to you. And you will seek me and find me, when you search for me with all your heart. I will be found by you, says the Lord, and I will bring you back from your captivity; I will gather you from all the nations and from all the places where I have driven you, says the Lord, and I will bring you to the place from which I cause you to be carried away captive." - Jeremiah 29:11-14

You are not going through hell for no reason. Lately it may seem as if your life is up in shambles. You don't know what you really want to do (career wise), your finances are all tied up, and you are feeling all alone. You've even considered giving up and your hope is at an all-time low. God is purposely making you uncomfortable in order to make you move! His purpose is greater than your understanding.

While we're waiting to do something important, God is doing something important in us and often, around us. He is refining us. He is making us uncomfortable. Dependent. He is revealing His strength in our weakness.

We can often find ourselves in familiar places, and yet, still feel on edge. My grandmother would say that's a "shifting in your spirit." It's God's way of communicating that where we are not our final landing. That He still has work for us to do so don't get comfortable where you are!

As you begin to earnestly pray and meditate be prepared for this shift! Too often we pray for God to remove obstacles and change situations, but when we hear Him speak and those commands become increasingly clear, we become too afraid to move! We become disgruntled and discontent with our lives. We become stuck in a cycle of complacency when God has greater waiting for us just around the corner.

Stepping out on faith is scary. However, I can say for certain that I've learned this important lesson: there can be no MANIFESTATION without MOVEMENT. God will do his part, he'll put t ht people in place, he'll provide you with the vision, and even connect you to multiple sources. The rest is up to you!

When God Gives Tests

"Blessed is the man who perseveres under trial; for once he has been approved, he will receive the crown of life, which the Lord has promised to those who love Him" (James 1:2-4,12)

God wants to see if we have learned what He has been teaching us. He rarely, if ever, announces them ahead of time. They just come. It might be a set of circumstances or a situation you will face to determine if you are really learning the material. God will test us to see if we are actually learning, growing, and advancing.

Sometimes we go through storms in life. Sometimes God will allow certain situations in our lives to test our faith. It is easy to say that you trust God, until you get a call from your doctor with some bad news, or until that person you are in love with breaks up with you, or until your job comes to an end.

These are tests.

When you are going through hardship or difficulty, sometimes it seems as though God has forgotten about you, that He is too busy. But God always has time for you. He loves you. God fully aware of what you are experiencing. Will you still trust Him even when things don't go your way — even when life doesn't unfold the way that you hoped it would? Will you trust God to see you through the storm?

Will you pass the test?

In the Meantime

e meantime is that waiting period between here and where you are destined to end up.

nsider an area of your life for which your vision looks cloudy. You don't know what you want, you just don't know what steps will be essential to take you where you want to go.

aiting for your right answer is an exercise in trusting God and letting go of your attempt to ntrol things. The truth is, we aren't in control anyway and we expend a lot of energy trying to ove to ourselves that we are.

op focusing on needing to know the answers. Focus on the message that is being offered to J in the process of learning what to do next.

hesians 3:20 says, "To Him who is able to do exceedingly, abundantly above all you could er think or imagine.

Personal Task:

What answer are you waiting on? What message is being offered to you right now? What area of your life do you need to focus on while you await your answer?

Write your area of focus below!

_____

_____

_____

_____

_____

_____

Living in the Moment

When I began this book, I mentioned a moment that proved significant in my personal growth. For my 32nd birthday, my friends got together and hosted a "Bikes and Brunch" event. It was an awesome day in which a group of beautiful women gathered together to enjoy a day of fun authenticity, love, and sisterhood! There would be no phones, no social media, or no outside distractions. Only love, conversation, and personal engagement allowed. We were truly "in the moment."

This hit me as I came to the realization that I'm always on the go, never allowing myself the opportunity to be in the moment. That's not the life I want for myself or my family. When I leave this world, I want to have experienced every ounce of what life has to offer; whatever that may be.

How can we possibly just be happy, be present, and enjoy our lives? How can we stop worrying about tomorrow and regretting yesterday? Well, the process itself is simple to understand, but like anything else in life, it takes conditioning. Fear and anxiety are concepts of the mind. The mind creates fear and anxiety, putting us into a state of distress. That's only because it's been conditioned to do that.

5 simple steps of daily habit development to live in the moment

- The first 5 to 10 minutes of your day should be devoted to daily gratitude. Make a conscious effort to literally "count your blessings" and intently focus on all of the positive things happening in your life.
- Develop the habit of physical activity. It's been scientifically proven that even 10 minutes of exercise a day can have a drastic impact on your mood and overall state of happiness. During exercise, your brain releases endorphins and other chemicals to combat stress. So not only will your physical health improve but your mental health as well! That's "winning" Sis!

Commit yourself to limiting your distractions during a specific block of time. Pick one small block of time, whether it's for an hour or as little as 15 minutes and detach yourself mentally and physically from the world. Turn off electronic devices (unless you're using a meditation app), don't answer those calls, and shut down that brain!

Find a way, every day, to give something to someone in need. It's important to remember that a blessing or gift doesn't have to involve money. Do a welfare check-in on a close friend or co-worker, pay it forward with lunch or coffee, smile at someone as you pass them in the hallway. It honestly doesn't take much to be impactful.

We're more focused on hate and pain rather than love and beauty. You can shift the tide. Find the beauty in something; anything. It doesn't matter what it is. Take a walk and listen to the birds chirping, or literally smell the flowers. It's the little things in life that will allow us to be happier and more present.

"Wherever you are be all there" Jim Elliot

"Being in the Moment"

Personal Task: Write about your most recent or most memorable experience of "being in the moment". Be as descriptive as possible (sights, smells, sounds…) allowing your mind to recapture that moment.

_____

_____

_____

_____

_____

_____

_____

_____

_____

_____

Pulse check! How are you feeling thus far on this journey?

Silent Seasons

"God is working behind the scenes in your life. His Silence is not His absence. He is behind the scenes like a Puppet Master pulling strings in your life!" - TD Jakes

In the spirit of transparency, let me express a personal challenge: I struggle with patience! I need to see immediate fruits of my labor or I begin to feel discouraged or second guess the decisions I've made or the paths I've chosen. Insecurities and self-doubt emerge from the shadows to rear their ugly heads. Maybe I should've waited to start that business. Perhaps I shouldn't have invested so much into that personal project. It's human nature and I will raise my hand to profess that I am a constant work in progress.

Sooner or later, you will be at a place when God is silent. You will be crying out for help, desperately praying for direction, and not receiving an answer in return.

Silent times are often God's means of preparing us for something greater. God's silence is never random or indifferent. These moments of silence are often not without sound reason. It could be that . . .

We're not ready to listen.

He wants to get our attention.

He is teaching us to trust Him.

He is using silence to mature us.

He wants us to persevere in prayer.

[?]

Who I'm Meant to Be

We are only a few steps away from the end of our journey together! Let's make sure we end strong! I wanted to share this quiz I came across on Oprah's website and thought it would be perfect to include in the book.

This quiz can help you figure out what really defines you

Who Am I Meant to Be?

http://www.oprah.com/inspiration/who-are-you-meant-to-be-self-assessment-quiz_1

sonal Task: Take the quiz and reflect on the results. Write a few sentences about your

lings.

_____

_____

_____

_____

_____

_____

_____

_____

Pain, Passion, and Purpose

"... And when it finally stops raining, you're going to see how God used the storm to help you grow!
Tera Carissa

They say God gives his toughest battles to his strongest soldiers, but the truth is, that's all of u
We are stronger than we think, but too often we don't believe we have the power to make it
through life's circumstances. I wouldn't be where I am today if I hadn't gone through some of
the things I have in life. While we all face opposition, everyone's stories and struggles are
completely unique. The battles we experience are what shape and mold us into the incredible
people we are and hold the key to who we have yet to become. There are many people who
have yet to reach their full potential either because they are afraid that they may actually be
great, or they don't have the strength to make it past their current circumstances. Most of life
difficult experiences truly take resilience and strength to withstand the storm.

While I've endured many life-changing events, my dad's death was one of the toughest, eye-
opening, heartbreaking, and trying times in my life. I remember going through a bad breakup
being down to my very last penny and losing my dad all in the same breath of a moment. I
thought to myself "this could not be life". Why my family, why my dad and why did my mom
have to be put in a position to lose the only man she'd ever loved? I experienced so many
emotions during this time as any normal person would; grief, anger... sadness. I found myself
questioning God and then apologizing for my questions. How dare I question God? Yet, I
wanted answers... I needed answers.

My dad's death shed light on a part of reality I wouldn't wish on any family. My siblings and I
were left to pick up so many pieces with a thousand of unanswered questions. Sometimes I s
pray, and talk to God, as well as my dad, somehow hoping to find those elusive answers, but
honestly that's a part of life no one can prepare you for. Sometimes there are no answers,
sometimes things happen in life and we'll never understand.

dad was the true definition of a soldier. Not only had he retired from the United States my, but he had served almost another 20 years overseas as a military contractor. He loved military life and was a patriot to his core. So, when he made the unexpected announcement he was returning home for good, I remember being initially shocked. That shock gave way suspicion as I thought to myself, "no way is he really giving up the life." I distinctly remember ving a conversation with my mom and expressing my concern that "something was up".

put this in perspective, during those years we only saw my dad approximately 30 days out of ear. Crazy right! Trust me I know that sounds insane, but that was our life and we went with flow of it each year. So, to hear that my dad was coming home for good; we knew that nething happened. Unfortunately, my dad kept the knowledge of the whys and the what den from us for six whole months, before his illness manifested in its entirety and could no ger be denied nor contained.

anuary 2015, God called my daddy home. My heart was broken, and my soul was shattered lose the first man I had ever loved.

wards the end of his life, my Dad was extremely sick and in so much pain. Yet, he consistently used medical attention... until it was too late to save him. At one point he even refused atment and transportation from an ambulance that my mom had called to their house in a ment of desperation.

another occasion, my brother and cousin drove to Columbus from Atlanta in order to vince my dad to seek treatment at the local military hospital. They were successful; vever, it was then that we received the severity of his prognosis: my dad had cirrhosis of the r and he would need a liver transplant to survive. But there was hope, at least we thought. dad was admitted into the hospital for a few days, but he constantly fought to be released. n's 5th birthday was coming up and he begged the nurses to release him in time to attend birthday party. Thankfully he was well enough to be released. I'm so glad he was able to be there. He was still sick and weak and very rarely moved out of one spot, but he was there. Littl did we know that 2 short weeks later he would no longer be with us.

The week following my dad's release from the hospital in Columbus, Georgia, he was schedule for a follow up visit at the prestigious Emory Hospital in Atlanta. Emory had recently gotten approved to treat liver failure using an experimental technique. My dad was in grave condition by then and the night before the appointment, he was in excruciating pain. When my mom, dad, and sister arrived for the follow up, doctors delivered even more devastating news: they could not treat my dad for his liver failure because his kidneys had also begun to shut down.

Instead of going for a simple treatment, my dad was admitted into the hospital on that Monday morning. Even though his prognosis seemed bleak by all standards, it never dawned us that my dad would not be leaving the hospital. We prayed, sang, and cried. I remember my brother playing all the good oldies for him, my sister playing spirituals for him, and my cousin singing for him. Even in the midst of tragedy, our family found a way to bond.

By Tuesday my dad was totally unresponsive. How could this be happening? Wednesday cam and then Thursday. I remember talking to my mom while I was at work and she mentioned th Palliative Care team being involved. I've never had to encounter a Palliative Care team so like any other person I googled it. At that moment I knew I had to leave work. My manager told n to just go and I'm so glad he did. Things were going downhill fast. The doctors said they would be moving my dad to hospice and making him comfortable. Everyone in the room began cryin That was the most devastating news ever. Questions still lingered. How did we get here? How did this go so very wrong? This man was not weak...he was a soldier who had survived Desert Storm and the bombing of the military compound in Riyadh. My daddy was a survivor and on of the strongest men I knew. He was going to pull through and prove them all wrong. It didn't matter that they were "elite" doctors. God wouldn't let my dad survive all of that just to die...like this.

day came. The hospital was filled with so much love and support from family, friends, the
ctors and the nurses on duty. The shallowed breaths of my dad greeted every entrance into
e room, but we still had faith. Because that's what we had been taught: God answers prayers.
d is a miracle worker. God has the last say.

en, one of the nurses said, "if you want to say your last good-byes, do them now". Then…it
s real. I'd never felt as weak as I did in that moment. My cousin Shavon literally had to catch
e from falling. This was not my reality.

en as he transitioned, my daddy fought. Until his very last breath he was a soldier. I
member the tears. I remember my mama's wails. My daddy was gone, officially gone. My
ther had lost the man she'd shared her life with since she was 14 years old. She was
vastated and in disbelief. Yet, I could barely comfort her as I was in the throes of the worst
n I'd ever experienced.

is the case of all human beings, my dad wasn't a perfect man. I loved him anyway. I would
e to think that if my dad still had time, he would've righted a lot of wrongs. He would've had
e conversations he should have had. And I believe he would've mended some brokenness he
d a hand in creating.

at I learned the most during this difficult time was to never think "you have enough time".
u should live each day as if these are your last moments and learn to not give energy to
ngs that won't matter weeks or even months from now. Use what time you have on this
th in its entirety. Don't ever take life for granted. Cherish your relationships, and
sistently express compassion and gratitude.

n't let life defeat you. Grief is a pain that cuts extremely deep. With time I found myself
in and I bounced back. I often talk about Iyanla Vanzant's incredible book "Peace from
ken Pieces". In this book Iyanla recounted some of her own spiritual lessons that happened

51

over the last decade in her life; from her failing marriage to losing her daughter to illness on Christmas Day. Iyanla's book truly taught me how to get through what I was going through. I bounced back with dignity, strength and resilience. I knew that this was a turning point in my life, a new beginning. I had to go through that time; God needed me to experience everything I did in that exact order.

Experience teaches us lessons that carry us through the journey of life. Through my dad's death, I learned to find purpose in my pain. Despite this horrible thing that happened in my life, I had to trust that God was still going to fulfill all the promises that he had for me.

Four years later and I am still on that journey. Yet, God continues to amaze me and has never forsaken me. I have a passion and purpose to ensure that I pour into the lives of people... to encourage and to uplift. To spread the message that the storm won't last always and if you just have a little faith and truly trust God he will come through on his promises, often, right in the nick of time.

I often tell God to use me up. I don't want one single minute to be wasted and certainly no talent to be unused. My dad spoke of his personal goals and ambitions; however, he put them aside in lieu of his responsibilities to his country. He was a soldier first and a man second. I wonder sometimes if the order of roles were reversed would he still be alive. Again, I'll have to settle for not knowing the answers.

It's taken some time but I'm finally coming to peace with that. My dad's journey and life were his. All I can do is to ensure that my own purpose is fulfilled.

As famously stated in a Robert Frost poem "I have promises to keep and miles to go before I sleep, and miles to go before I sleep."

Making Mommy Moves

"Being a mother...is learning about strengths you didn't know you had and dealing with fears you didn't know existed"-Linda Wooten

cliché as it may sound, my son Camden has been one of my greatest blessings. I remember en I first found out I was pregnant. I had just come back from Spring Break in Miami and well 's just say your girl was one of those who had a "missed month."

rvous, out of my mind, and scared as hell, I decided to take a solo trip to the Kennesaw State iversity (KSU) clinic where I received the news that would change the projection of my life. om! Just like that, I was a whole 8 weeks pregnant. Yes, I cried. I was shocked and appointed in my circumstances and didn't know how in the hell I was going to tell my folks. I s a senior in college and knew that the pregnancy could impact my timeline for graduation. many crazy thoughts spun through my head. I finally mustered up enough nerves to spill the ws to my mom and sister, fearing the disappointment that I was sure was awaiting me. Their ictions were totally unexpected. From the moment I told them they were happy, excited, and couraging. Before I could make any personal decisions, they immediately stated "don't even nk about an abortion!" It wasn't anything I had even considered, but they wanted to enforce concept that it wasn't even an option. I remember my sister mentioning not being able to ve kids and that we would make sure we brought this little one into the world as "ours". Even m the beginning, the village was an integral part of our existence.

10 knew then at 8 weeks just how much of a light this kid would be, not only to me, but to so ny others? Now don't get me wrong, like any other kid there are times this little joker tests entire sanity. Still I wouldn't trade my boy for the world. Being a mom by far has been one the most challenging, trying, yet rewarding experiences of all times and, if given a choice, I uld always choose to do it over again.

Believe me when I say I've seen the struggle. I've gone through quite a few challenging experiences being a single mom, but I thank God for each and every one of those experiences. needed each one to get me to where I am today.

Driving down 75 one night, I called my mom crying and bawling hysterically (sis couldn't stop). Life was hard and I just wanted to make it. I wanted to make it past being a single mom, I wanted to make it past living paycheck to paycheck, I wanted to make it past trying to rely on people to do what it was they were supposed to do. Hell, I just wanted to make it past being down to my very last. Life was hard, money was tight, and bills were unyielding. I was at a point where I seriously thought I wouldn't and couldn't survive. I wanted to give up. I was tired. I needed help, financially and spiritually.

That night my mom prayed with me and most importantly, FOR me. I felt a renewed energy in my spirit. Once I calmed down somewhat, she encouraged me to pray for MYSELF. From that day forward I prayed harder than what I would typically pray. A funny thing happened: God began to work in and through me and restored my faith experience by experience, day by day.

As many women have, I went through an unhealthy cycle with men. At the time, my greatest struggle was expecting Cam's father to be who I wanted, and we needed him to be. The fact that I wasn't getting what I felt we deserved almost drove me insane. At that time, my sister told me something profound that changed my entire perspective, "Only God can change the hearts of man". Those words struck a chord with me. For so long I had worked entirely too hard to force not only my child's father but others in my life into this box that I had created for them in my mind. In reality, people are who they are. We have a choice to accept and engage with their personalities and behaviors or not. We can love extra hard, give way too much and it still won't change a person. Their own life journeys must bring them to a point of transformation. Only God has the power to transform. And I am NOT God!

, I made the only decision I could. I moved out of God's way and prayed that things would
ft and change. Not so much for me, but for my son. I learned the hard way that hurt people,
rt people and people can't give you what they don't have.

spite being a single mom (a single mom of a son at that) the kid has never lacked or gone
thout. I learned in my early years of motherhood that it takes a village to raise a child. And by
d, he showed out with mine. It was the times when I felt like I couldn't and wouldn't make it
my own that they showed up and showed out for me the most. I had friends who didn't
en have kids jumping into the rotation to lend a helping hand. My sister Kinia and brother-in-
/ Theo would catch a flight at the drop of the dime... just to simply show up and be present.
brother, on one occasion, turned around halfway to work just to be sure the kid had
neone in attendance for "Donuts with Dad". My cousin-in-law Norris and my partner Jay are
ner male figures who show up! For at least 2 years, my cousins Shavon and Norris made sure
kid, along with their own, were good after school (sounds simple, but being a single mom
s was a big deal). I had Granny and GiGi who always, always made sure the kid was straight. I
ld go on and on but trust me when I say there just aren't enough pages to give each
ividual their just due. Forgive me if I don't mention each gesture, but I'm always grateful for
village.

. here I am today. I made it past that ugly cry of a night on 75. God gifted me with the most
azing village and future husband. Yes, future husband! Yes, I am claiming it! I made it past
ng a single mom because I am more than that. Five years later, I am an employee of a
tune 500 company with two successful businesses under my belt. I am a Published
otographer, I've been featured twice on VoyageATL, I am a mom-preneur and now I can
cially add "Published Author" to my list of accomplishments.

as not come without trials. You would think that with two businesses, I would have it down
, but that's not the case...AT ALL. Finding that balance is still a daily struggle. Just being
om" comes with challenges that I'm sure many of us face. Between transports, homework

(this new math is the devil in disguise), sports and other activities, there's very little room for personal and bonding time, much less time for business. After Cam is in bed, you will find me packaging wraps and jewelry, editing photos, checking emails, and creating social media content. I'm second guessing myself most of the time and exhausted all the time.

My advice to all moms/mom-preneurs out there ready to throw in the towel; cry if you must but have faith in knowing that the storm won't last always. God will fulfill every promise he ha for you. I pray that you are inspired by my own personal testimony and that in your personal life you find the peace that surpasses all understanding. Know that even when you can't see t light at the end of the tunnel, it's still there.

Hold fast Sis!

⍰

Building, Branding, Business

t me be really clear...entrepreneurship is not for the weak of heart. Do I need to say it louder ⁺ the people in the back? There are a lot of long and sleepless nights perfecting and crafting ur brand. It is a whole different level of stepping out on faith. You must be willing to commit, ᵉest, and take a loss and even if no one else does. You must be willing to take a chance on urself...even if no one else does.

ᵉating an effective brand takes years of hard work, dedication, and nonstop working. Building ⁻usiness is one thing, ensuring the longevity and profitability of that business requires years ᵉestablishing your reputation and brand. The more you grow the more growing pains you will ᶜounter. However, you will learn what works and what doesn't work for your brand and ᵇiness and even then there will be times when you'll have to adapt and change along the y.

ᵇwing pains are real! No matter how prepared you think you are, things can, and will, go ᵇng and not according to plan. For someone with control issues (raises hand to the sky) that ⁿ be, and was, very difficult to handle.

ᵇhough people knew me and my work ethic, I felt as though I constantly had to prove myself ᵈ my worth, especially in the beginning. I've experienced a client not liking my photos. I've ᵇerienced not getting support. I was once hired for a party where everything from the ᵐnera, the lighting, the Wi-Fi that could go wrong WENT WRONG. In that early stage I ᵘggled with editing, time management, and scheduling. I did not have any kind of strategic ᵉn and it made the journey and the work that much harder. I had the creativity, the vision, ᵈ the talent; what I failed to have was a strong foundation or business plan that enabled me ᵇave a functioning, profitable business. Indeed, it was not a smooth road, but a string of ᵇrning curves and lessons. I learned to embrace every moment.

*****

As a photographer, my most challenging shoot was my first wedding. Like any challenging situation you must get your feet wet and you truly don't know what to expect or what it's real like until you're right smack in the moment. I was lucky in that my client and her family were amazing and accommodating. They really made my first wedding a great encounter. It was a 1 hour wedding day for me and I went solo (big lesson learned). I started my morning at 7:00 a. shooting the bride and bridesmaid getting their makeup done and ended the night around 9:0 p.m. with the final send off. Prior to shooting of course I researched, studied lighting and prepared myself as much I knew how to do so. I made sure I had enough memory for my SD card, extra batteries, and an external flash.

The videographer on hand was extremely helpful and we partnered together to ensure we were clear of each other's shots. 12 grueling hours later the event was a wrap. Little ol me ha survived her first solo shoot! I walked away with so much more knowledge than ever before. I share with you some of my "takeaways" from that experience that can be utilized in all forms business:

1. Set expectations
2. Decide on a pricing structure
3. Be Realistic--Personally, I knew that I would never shoot another 12-hour day, lord help me, and definitely not solo.
4. Be Prepared! – On the day of the shoot I learned these fundamental photography rules:
   - I learned the importance of a having a shot list and the extra accessories to always have on hand
   - It is extremely important with a larger wedding to have a second shooter on hand and even gain second shooter experience yourself prior to.
   - Scout the venue before the day of the wedding
   - Prepare for the weather

5. Relax -Even though some things may not go according to plan, you still have the ability to create a lasting experience.

▪ying organized proved critical for me to keep myself from being overwhelmed and feeling

t. I was able to enjoy what I loved doing while interacting with the family at the same time.

at one opportunity has in turn landed me 15+ amazing wedding and engagement

portunities alone, not including those that I had to pass up or refer to other colleagues due

booking conflicts. I know without a doubt that if I would've never taken that opportunity, I

uld not have had the opportunities that followed.

Moving On Up

It's been a few years now and I'm still on this entrepreneurial journey where I'm evolving and thriving more as each day passes. My best advice to anyone starting out on the journey to entrepreneurship and starting a business is to be genuine, authentic and consistent. There will be 1000 people who set out on this same journey and of those 1000 maybe a 100 (or more) will have the same brand idea as you and even more won't survive. Don't stop, give up or get discouraged. Know what makes your brand stand out.

I want to share a personal story with you about a business situation that illustrates this point.

Right before the launch of my Issa Wrap Inspired Collection, I received a cease and desist notice via email from a company claiming I had "stolen" their name and brand. Yep! I'm sure your mouths dropped just as mine did at the time. At first, I was nervous and somewhat taken aback because I was literally getting ready to launch and had just begun promoting my new brand. I knew I had done my research on the name and of course there are a ton of creatively named head wrap companies out, but I knew that I had specifically done the work on my brand name and it was available. Before responding, I reached out to my sister and brother in law who respectively have years of experience in the business and tech field. Just to give you some background, my sister is a force to be reckoned with! Once I explained what was going on, she did what she does best...went to work! No one messes with her babies!

After hours of research and phone calls she learned enough to conclude that I was in good standing and was not guilty of any violations. As business owners there are key things to remember; know the business, do the work, and research, research, RESEARCH! Especially in this age of social media where your online presence has the potential to grow and reach thousands of people.

Here are a few additional tips to keep in mind. Please note that this information is based on Georgia law. Check with your respective states to determine qualifications and requirements

cide on a Legal Structure:
1. The most common legal structures for a small business are:
   a. Sole Proprietorship
   b. Partnership
   c. Limited Liability Company (LLC), and Corporation

oose a Name:
1. For LLCs and corporations, you will need to check that your name is different from the names of other business entities already on file with the Georgia Secretary of State.
2. You can check for available names by doing a business search on the Georgia Secretary of State website.
3. You can reserve an available name for 30 days by filing a name reservation request with the Georgia Secretary of State either online through the ecorp website or on paper with a Name Reservation Request form. There is a $25 fee associated with name reservations.

ate Your Business Entity:
1. It is important to know what documents are needed based on the legal structure you decide to go with.

ain, this is basic information to consider before getting fully involved in creating your

siness. Learn what you can when you can, and feel free to connect with a business mentor or

attorney if it's too overwhelming. It's always better to be safe than sorry and you don't want

nvest time, energy, and money without fully doing your due diligence.

en the dust settled, we were two different businesses providing similar products utilizing

ilar brand names. Further research proved that the business challenging my existence was

ually dissolved a few years before. Go figure.

entially, I said all this to say - don't let anyone try to discourage you or defeat you. If my

er had not done the research, and if the company had not emailed me, I would have

nestly not known about a cease and desist order. Now, more than ever I'm cautious of

uring that the research doesn't stop and that I continue to learn the ins and outs of the

siness world including the rules of copyrights and trademarks. Being an entrepreneur is a

tty big deal and requires a lot of footwork. You must be willing to put in the work, Point

nk Period.

*****

Thinking about the future keeps me motivated and excited. No matter where I am today, despite how far I've gotten, I am sure to continue to go far. It has been an exciting journey branding my name and building my businesses. When people hear about, see the names of, read about Yasmin Watts, Yasmin Watts Photography or Issa Wrap Inspired Collection, I want them to draw inspiration not only from the pictures I capture but through my personal stories and experiences as well. I want to provide a platform for all women and motivate them to pursue their life and business goals.

My personal goals are to someday have an opportunity to shoot celebrities and major events like the BET Awards and the Grammys. I would also like to be featured in Essence or other lifestyle magazines. When I first started, those goals seemed so vast and impossible. Yet, my work has led to opportunities beyond what I could have initially imagined. I've had the opportunity for my work to go viral on social media as well as for my kid clients to be featured in magazines. I've worked with businesses like March of Dimes for the March for Babies Walk and Piedmont Healthcare for the Heart Walk in 2017. I've been hired as a contracted photographer for major brands. One experience, one event, one step of faith at a time...from impossible to possible.

*****

Making the choice to add another stream of income and launch Issa Wrap Inspired Collection came to full life after a 21- Day Dream Challenge with Tiara Johnson who is a Dream Coach in Atlanta. This challenge was absolutely amazing to me and everything I needed to hold myself accountable. During that challenge I had the opportunity to identify my target audience, develop a mission and brand, and be clear on how my product would impact the world. That journey led to the execution of my official launch party; which was incredible by the way.

One important lesson to learn in business is that no matter what you think you know, someone else will always know more! As such, don't ever be too proud to reach out for mentorship and dance. Take that class, attend that workshop, listen in on that webinar, join that business up. Staying connected and establishing a solid circle of entrepreneurs and experts from all ds is the real BOSS move.

*****

Congrats Sis! You've put in the work; you've done all the legwork and the paperwork; you are now officially an entrepreneur. Now it's time to start thinking strategically about how to ensu that your business is a successful venture. That process starts with branding yourself to the public.

What exactly is "branding?" That word is tossed around quite a bit in the world of entrepreneurship. Some would say that branding is synonymous with marketing. It's your strategy on how to present your business and product to the public so that it stands out amor other businesses and products. Essentially, your brand is your business identity. It's your message, your mission and your values all wrapped up in one pretty marketing package. A ke component of developing your brand is determining who your target audience is and in what ways are you trying to connect with them.

It's also important to realize that YOU are your brand. You are your greatest asset when it comes to brand building. If you haven't heard it before, you'll hear it from me: people don't ji purchase products, they buy into who you are as a person, your personal identity and personality.

I've heard many entrepreneurs complain about an overall lack of support from family, friends and others. I must say that I don't have that complaint. There are times when I've actually be overwhelmed by the totality of love and support that I received from those directly in my circ as well as those connected to my circle by some indirect means (friends of friends, friends of family...). What I've learned is when people believe in you and feel a connection with you, the will support you. It's their own way of investing in you.

That being said, being in a state of "mindfulness" is essential once you become an entrepreneur. You should always be mindful of your message, mindful of your connections, conversations and your daily interactions with people as a whole. You never know who is

64

nnected to who, who has the potential to be your next customer or who may even have the tential to be an investor! God will place people and opportunities in your path for your good; wever, I'm a firm believer that you can surely block your blessings. The next time you mplain about a lack of support, check yourself Sis! Check your attitude, your relationships (or k thereof). Check your actions and your reactions. You may just be surprised at what you d.

Social Media Marketing and Strategies

"You are responsible for everything you post and everything you post is a reflection of you

-Germany Kent

One of the greatest tools available in getting your brand nationally and internationally recognized is social media access. The development of social media platforms changed the game in the world of business! Whereas entrepreneurs had to previously depend on "word of mouth", local advertisements, and grassroots efforts in order to generate awareness about their business, brands and products, with social media you can literally reach thousands of potential customers while sitting in the comfort of your own living room. Social media engagement and social media content are important terms to remember and understand when it comes to marketing, branding and promoting. Social media engagement involves how you interact with your "audience"—which includes other users, other entrepreneurs, and potential connects/customers. Social media content refers to the information, promotions, and messages you provide on your social media platform. Your social media content is critical in reaching your audience and inviting engagement.

Here are some strategic questions to consider when creating social media content:

- Is your content engaging? (daily posts...)
- Is your content on target with your brand?
- Does your content evoke emotion?
- Are your images inviting?
- Is your content relevant?
- Are you utilizing the platform to its full potential (hashtags, ads)

Remember, your social media platform is an extension of who you are as an entrepreneur. You are promoting your brand and selling not only your products but yourself. Your image matters. The right social media campaigns/promotions can successfully generate revenue, awareness, and hype for your business. Do your research and make social media work for you.

*****

with all things, social media does have a downside. While it can be an effective marketing
ol in a professional sense; personally, it can too often prove to be a curse. With social media
vitably taking over everyone's lives, interactions and engagements have changed
amatically and will continue to do so. Social media can be utilized to both motivate and
pire people on different paths especially in business; but unfortunately, it has been used in
ister ways to bully and shame. As humans we also tend to fall into the pitfall of comparison.
cial media, and the windows it provides to other people's worlds, can leave us feeling
fulfilled and unworthy. It's a difficult road to balance.

matter how good things look on the outside, we all face the same struggles and insecurities
the next person. When you look at social media, most of the time it involves people posting
ly the best of themselves. However, many of us have probably come to realize, no one's life
erfect.

e yourself grace to be perfectly imperfect no matter what you see going on around you. We
st stop believing everything we see. Behind every perfectly curated Instagram feed or
ebook profile, is a person who may be just as insecure as you are. They could be just as
ved and feel just as lonely sometimes. In the social media world, they may be health food
kies and fitness geeks, while, in reality, they are over-indulging on sugar, eating almond
tter straight from the jar and consuming convenient pre-packaged treats. Probably a lot, too.

challenge is to see these images and recognize them for what they truly represent: small
le snapshots of a whole life. These social media feeds may portray illusions of perfection, but
lives they represent are not. How do I know that? Because no one's life is! Life is more than
a series of pretty pictures. It's ALL of the perfectly imperfect moments in between. A friend
e said, "if everyone put all of their problems in a basket, and saw the full scope of other
ple's problems, we would be quick to take ours back." I've found this to hold a lot of truth.

I've had moments where I've had to remind myself of just how much I love my imperfect life. Especially when I hear people speak on some of the troubles they've gone through or are currently going through. Moments of reflection can make us "grateful" for the problems we d we have in comparison to others.

I recall a moment sitting in church, listening to a guest preacher speak about loss. He spoke in detail about losing his Godmother in one week and then losing his Mom in the very next week. Then, during the planning of his mom's funeral he lost his best friend and still, three weeks lat his sister. Even in his state of despair, he committed to conduct the eulogies for them all. The congregation became emotional as he recounted how the same hands he used to pray and lif in praise to God were the same ones used to close his loved ones' caskets. It was unfathomab pain than I could not imagine to that scale. My state of gratefulness expanded as I listened to him speak. My life has certainly had its moments of tragedy, joy, love, pride and craziness. Eve still, I'm thankful for it ALL.

Thank you, God for this imperfect life just as it is.

So, the next time you compare yourself to someone else or look at the imperfections in your own life take a moment to breathe and reflect— What's beautiful? What's good? What's new What's inspiring you right now (or what could inspire you if you allowed it to)?
Beauty is all around you if you know where to look.

🔲

Are You Ready?

at's such a loaded question, right? I'm sure blood pressures and anxiety levels just elevated ough the roof. Change is scary. Taking new steps is scary. Hopefully this guide has served its rpose of getting you started on your personal journey to manifesting your dreams and eashing that inner BOSS that's been bursting to get out. What's important to remember is at everyone's journey is unique. Don't allow the process to overwhelm you. It's ok to tread tly, taking one baby step at a time. The point is to start!

let's wind (wine if you prefer) down and recap some key points from our journey.

- **Manifestation and Mindfulness**: External changes can only occur when there are changes within. No matter what your goal is, losing weight, starting a business...in order to truly be successful, your heart, mind, and spirit must first be aligned. It's then that you are your most powerful and creative self. Pray and meditate with intention.

- **The Endgame**: Before beginning your journey, determine exactly what your goal/s are. Your endgame may not be to start a new business and that's ok. It could be earning a degree, getting a certification or changing relationships and habits. Whatever your endgame is, know that you have the power to manifest it.

- **Research**: Being spontaneous in life can be exciting. However, when it comes to business it's not always a good thing to just jump in head-first without testing the waters. Do your research on costs, trends, state regulations, trademarks! Minimize the element of surprise as they can be costly in the long run.

- **Develop a Strategic Plan**: A strategic plan is a way of developing and organizing your overall goals and mission. This plan may change over time, but it can provide a great starting point. A good strategic plan should also include areas of strengths and those that need improvement in order to obtain your goals.

- **Create an Action Plan**: Not only should you know what your endgame is, you should create a plan that outlines the necessary steps to achieve your goal. You won't ever get a degree without first enrolling or filing for financial aid if needed. Remember, no manifestation can happen without ACTION. Every action counts as one step closer to your dream.

- **Build Your Brand**: It's a new day. In modern times, word of mouth will only get you so far. It's almost impossible to generate a certain level of success without establishing or online presence. Develop that website, create your social media profiles. Just remember to be mindful of what you present. In the world of entrepreneurship your greatest asset is YOURSELF. Every post and image represent who are and what your brand stands for Show the world that you are worth the investment!

- **Network**: If you're the smartest person in your circle, then you need a new circle! The journey of entrepreneurship is a long one. Prepare for the long-haul. Don't hesitate to collaborate with other individuals who are on the same journey. There's so much knowledge to be shared and insight to be gained if we just seek it out. Become a vend seek mentorship, take that workshop or class. Bet on yourself!

*****

As one chapter ends...a new one begins. The time to start your personal journe is NOW. Boss UP!

ray that this book touches you in ways you could've never imagined, that you learn to honor yourself and your space in the universe and learn to believe that the universe and God are working things out in your favor.

ll you have to do is make room for your blessing. As I always tell Cam, "What you put into the universe, is what comes back to you." Allow yourself the opportunity to be vulnerable, to dig deep and uproot the very things you tried to bury.

Let go, be free, and live a life of intent and purpose.

WE are coming for everything GOD's got for US!

SMIN WATTS is a native of Columbus, Georgia who currently resides in Atlanta, Georgia. She he proud parent of Camden Gibson, her nine-year-old son. A true Girl Boss, she is the ner/CEO of Yasmin Watts Photography and Issa Wrap Inspired Wrap Collection. Yasmin is o one of the Co-Founders of the STEAM based non-profit organization Abstract Village.

owerhouse on the rise, Yasmin has collaborated on several projects with esteemed npanies including BLOSSOM, March for Babies, Piedmont Healthcare, Yes Women on the e and Flapdoodles. She is the recipient of the 2018 Girl Boss Award for Best Photographer 1. She has been featured in Voyage ATL and Watch Blossom. Girl Boss is Yasmin's first rney into authorship. She has several upcoming Girl Boss workshops in the works.

Connect with Yasmin Watts:

Websites:

https://linktr.ee/yasminwattsphotography

https://www.yasminwattsphotography.com

https://www.issawrapcollection.com

Social Media:

Instagram: @yasminwattsphotography

@issawrapinspiredcollection

Facebook:

Yasmin Watts Photography

Issa Wrap Inspired Collection

Made in the USA
Columbia, SC
18 January 2020

86762086R00045